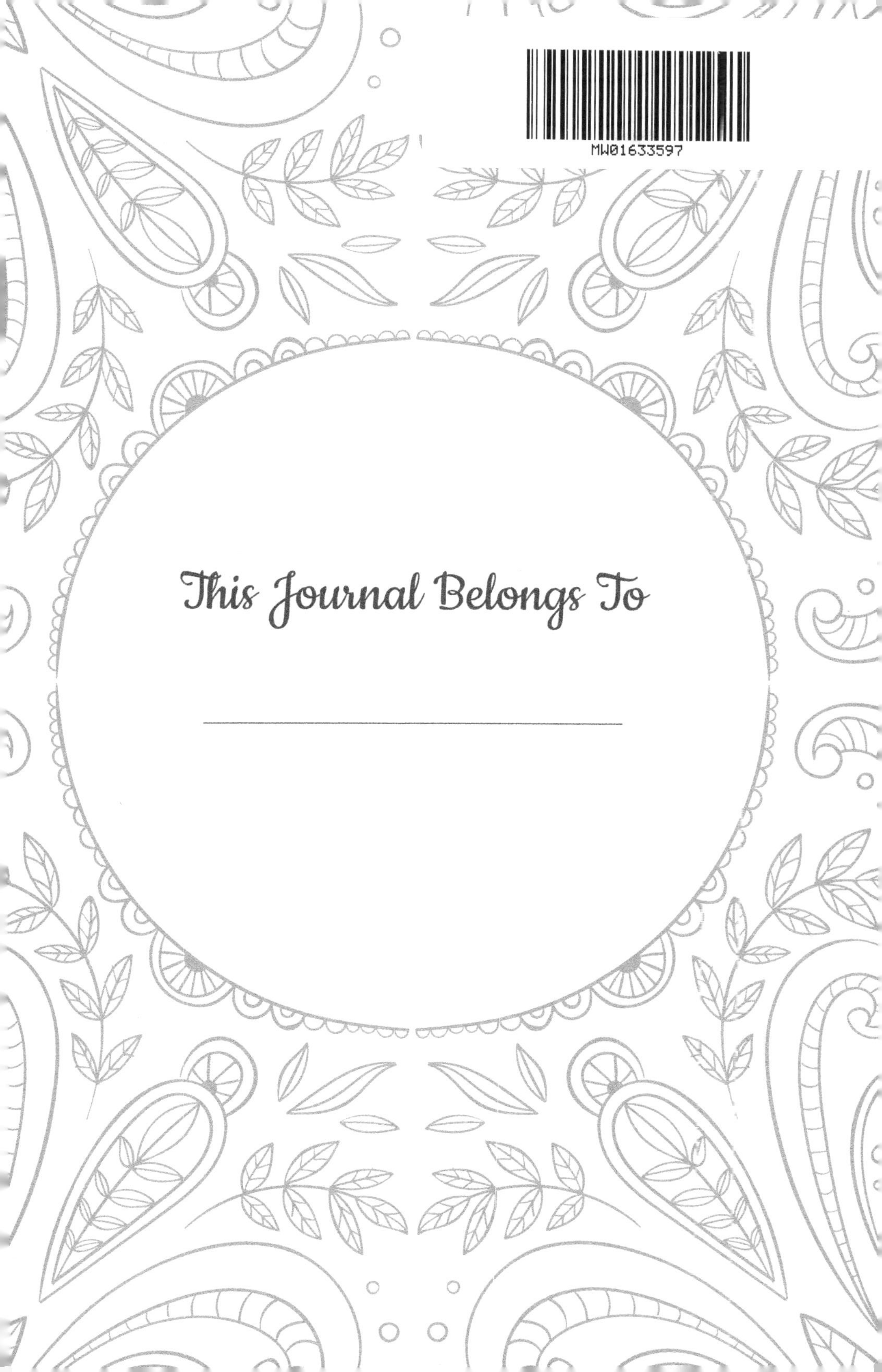
MW01633597
This Journal Belongs To

ISBN: 978-1-80101-234-8

Printed in the United States of America

First Edition

Introduction

Welcome to "Mom, Spill the Beans!"—a journal that celebrates not just the big moments but also every funny slip-up and happy surprise in your amazing journey as a mom. This isn't just another journal; it's a call to share the laughs, the turns of events that you didn't see coming, and all the joyful chaos that comes with being you.

Whether you're the mom who once turned baking a cake into a science experiment or the queen of funny stories that leave everyone laughing, this book is made for you. Filled with a little chaos and a lot of fun, this journal gives you the space to showcase the humor in your everyday life.

Inside, you'll find prompts that encourage you to share not just the smooth stories you'd tell at a party, but also the quirky, embarrassing, and downright strange moments you might otherwise forget. From childhood adventures and teenage mishaps to those unique "mom moments," we've set the scene for you to paint your life in bold, hilarious colors.

This book is a celebration—a vibrant collection of memories that make you uniquely you. It's designed to spark laughter and show a glimpse of the real woman behind the title 'Mom.' As you turn each page, challenge yourself to dig deeper and share those precious stories hidden in the corners of your memory.

So grab a pen, and let's fill these pages with your stories. Your family will cherish this funny keepsake, laughing all the way. This is more than just a journal; it's a legacy of laughter, a true snapshot of the life you've lived and loved.

Get ready to laugh, look back, and maybe, just maybe, spill the beans like never before. Every mom has her stories, and now it's time for yours to be told with all the joy they deserve.

Welcome to your story, told in a way only you can!

How to Spill the Beans Right

Welcome to your journey of laughter and heartfelt sharing! Here's how to make the most of your "Mom, Spill the Beans" journal:

Find Your Happy Place

Grab your favorite drink, find a cozy corner, and pick up a pen. This is your time to relax and explore your memories.

Let It All Out

Don't hold back. Embrace everything from the hilarious to the awkward. The more honest you are, the more engaging your stories will be.

Dive Into the Prompts

Each prompt is a door to your past. Go deep into the how and the why, not just the what and the when. Share not only what happened but also how you felt and what you learned.

Laugh at Yourself

Some of the best moments come from being able to laugh at our own blunders. Enjoy these humorous memories and let them shine in your stories.

Go With the Flow

Don't worry about order. Jump to any story that calls out to you, following wherever your mood takes you.

Enjoy the Sharing

Whether you keep it personal or involve family and friends, sharing these memories can add more layers of joy and laughter, especially with those who were part of the experiences.

Keep It Up

Regularly add to your journal to keep the narrative vibrant. Whether daily, weekly, or monthly, find a rhythm that keeps you engaged.

Pass It On

Once complete, your journal will be a treasure trove of laughter and wisdom. Think about passing it on to your children or grandchildren, letting your legacy of laughter continue.

Follow these steps to create not just a record, but a celebration of your life's unique journey through motherhood. Enjoy every moment of capturing and treasuring these memories!

CHAPTER 1:

Childhood Tricks

What was your favorite sneaky snack as a child?

Share the tale of a secret hideout you had.

What was the most creative excuse you made to skip school?

Describe a time you tried to fix something but ended up breaking it worse.

What was your favorite cartoon, and why did it make you laugh?

Who was your imaginary friend, and what adventures did you have?

Did you have a pet that helped you get into trouble?

How did you lose your first tooth?

What was the silliest game you created with your friends?

Tell us about your most memorable Halloween costume.

What was your biggest mess during arts and crafts?

What did you think clouds were made of?

Share a funny misunderstanding you had about adults.

What was your go-to trick for staying up past bedtime?

Who was your partner in crime and what did you get up to together?

Describe a funny moment with your first pet.

What was the most outrageous outfit you convinced your parents to let you wear?

Tell us about a time you made up a wild story and everyone believed it.

What was your least favorite chore, and how did you avoid doing it?

Share a memorable field trip mishap.

What was your secret talent as a kid?

Tell about a time you thought you'd discovered something great.

What was the worst haircut you got and how did you react?

What was your favorite silly song or rhyme?

Describe a time you tried to cook or bake something on your own.

What was the most interesting "treasure" you found and kept?

How did you help your family or friends with a funny scheme?

What was your favorite funny book or story?

Share a time you were scared but it turned out to be funny.

What was the most imaginative game you played?

CHAPTER 2: Teenage Antics

Share your most memorable sporting event blunder.

What was the biggest fashion faux pas you committed?

Describe your funniest memory involving a first car.

What was the most awkward situation you found yourself in with your crush?

Share the funniest thing that happened at a sleepover.

What was the biggest cooking disaster you had as a teenager?

Describe a time you got lost with friends.

Share a funny story about a teenage job you had.

Describe a prank call you made or received.

What was the silliest argument you had with a friend?

What was the most bizarre trend you participated in?

Describe your funniest moment at a family gathering.

Share your most comedic moment in a classroom.

What was your funniest encounter with a teacher or coach?

Describe a school project that went hilariously wrong.

What was the most ridiculous outfit you wore to a themed event?

Share a time when you tried a DIY beauty treatment and it backfired.

What was the silliest misunderstanding you had about the opposite sex?

Describe a funny mix-up with your schoolwork or homework.

What was the most outrageous excuse you used to get out of trouble?

Share your funniest attempt at a romantic gesture.

What was the most embarrassing thing your parents caught you doing?

Share a hilarious moment from prom or a school dance.

What was your biggest "I've got this" moment that totally backfired?

What was the funniest fashion statement you tried to make?

CHAPTER 3:

Love and Mischief

What was the funniest pickup line used on you or by you?

Share the most bizarre date you ever went on.

Describe a romantic gesture that was hilariously misunderstood.

What was the most awkward encounter with an ex?

Share a story about a funny misunderstanding with your partner.

What was the most absurd thing you did for love?

Describe a time you tried to make a romantic meal and it ended in disaster.

What was the funniest date you ever went on?

Share a comical moment from an anniversary.

What was the most awkward romantic advice you received?

What was the silliest fight you and your partner ever had?

Share a time when trying to be sexy went comically wrong.

What was the most bizarre romantic gift you ever received?

Describe a Valentine's Day that didn't go according to plan.

What was the funniest way you tried to impress a date?

Share your most humorous moment during an engagement or proposal.

What was the silliest misunderstanding you had about marriage?

Describe a time you were caught in a romantic mishap.

What was the funniest way you revealed your feelings to someone?

Share a story about a date where everything went wrong.

What was the most amusing conversation you had about relationships?

Describe your most awkward moment with someone you were attracted to.

What was the funniest way you tried to break up with someone?

Share the most humorous moment from a honeymoon.

What was the silliest thing you argued about with your partner?

Describe a time when a romantic surprise didn't go as planned.

What was the funniest reaction you had to a love song?

Share a story about a romantic gesture that was more funny than romantic.

What was the most awkward encounter you had with your partner's family?

Describe the funniest miscommunication you had on a date.

What was the silliest way you tried to win someone back?

Share your most humorous misunderstanding about dating.

What was the funniest outcome of trying to fix a relationship issue?

CHAPTER 4:

Parenting Bloopers

What was the funniest thing your child ever mispronounced?

Share a story about a time your parenting advice went hilariously wrong.

Describe your most chaotic moment in public with your kids.

What was the funniest reason you had to call a parent-teacher meeting?

Share your most comical holiday disaster with the family.

What was the most bizarre thing your child insisted on wearing?

Describe a time you tried a parenting hack and it failed spectacularly.

What was the funniest thing your child did at a family event?

Share a story about a time your child said something embarrassing in public.

What was the most comical mix-up during a family vacation?

Describe your funniest moment at a school function.

What was the silliest thing your child was convinced of?

Share a time when trying to take a perfect family photo went wrong.

What was the most absurd thing your child wanted for their birthday?

Describe a time you tried to teach your child something and it backfired.

What was the funniest misunderstanding you had about parenting before you had kids?

Share the most comical thing your child destroyed.

What was the silliest thing you did to get your child to sleep?

Describe a time your child's homework made you laugh.

What was the funniest thing your child ever brought home from school?

Share a story about a time your child tried to cook.

What was the most amusing way you discovered your child was up to no good?

Describe your most humorous attempt at disciplining your child.

What was the silliest costume your child chose for Halloween?

Share the funniest way your child tried to avoid doing chores.

What was the most bizarre pet your child wanted?

Describe a time your child gave you a funny explanation for something they did.

What was the funniest thing your child ever said about your job?

Share a story about a time your child misunderstood a family tradition.

What was the silliest reason your child ever gave for needing something new?

Describe your funniest travel mishap with kids.

What was the most absurd thing your child thought you were capable of?

Share your most humorous moment while teaching your child to drive.

What was the funniest thing your child said about growing up?

What was the most ridiculous excuse your child ever gave for not doing their homework?

Describe the funniest bath time saga with your kids.

What was the strangest fear your child had?

Share the most comical art project your child brought home.

What was the funniest reaction your child had to a new sibling?

Describe your child's most hilarious public dance or singing performance.

What's the most absurd rule your child insisted everyone at home follow?

Share a time your child misinterpreted a common saying or phrase.

What was the funniest outfit your child put together for a pet?

Describe a time your child took a family game way too seriously.

What's the silliest question your child ever asked about the world?

Share the funniest thing your child packed for a sleepover.

What was your child's most illogical explanation for a mess they made?

Describe a time your child was hilariously over-dramatic about a minor injury.

What's the most unexpected thing your child said they wanted to be when they grew up?

CHAPTER 5:

Oops Moments

Share a story about a DIY disaster at home.

What was the funniest cooking mistake you made that you tried to serve anyway?

Describe a time you tried to use modern technology and it went hilariously wrong.

What was the most embarrassing thing you said in a meeting or at work?

Share a time you thought you were texting one person but it went to someone else.

What was your biggest "oops" moment at a party?

Describe your most memorable wardrobe malfunction.

What was the funniest misunderstanding during a phone call?

Share a story about a time you locked yourself out of the house or car.

What was the funniest thing you've ever dropped or broken?

Describe your most embarrassing moment with a neighbor.

What was the most ridiculous mix-up with a reservation or appointment?

Share a time when you tried to be handy and ended up calling a professional.

What was the most comical injury you sustained doing something simple?

Describe a time you completely misunderstood directions.

What was the funniest mistake you made while traveling?

Share the most humorous miscommunication you had with a foreign language.

What was the biggest blunder you made while trying to impress someone?

Describe the most amusing encounter with an animal.

What was the funniest thing that happened at a wedding?

Share a story about a time you were completely unprepared for a significant event.

What was the most embarrassing thing you did while on a date?

Describe your funniest moment in public transportation.

What was the silliest argument you accidentally started?

Share the funniest thing you misinterpreted from a conversation.

What was the most ridiculous reason you were ever late?

Describe a time you tried to be sneaky and failed miserably.

What was your biggest "no way that just happened" moment?

Share a story about a funny mix-up with names.

What was the most absurd situation you found yourself in while trying to be polite?

Describe your most comical computer or technology fail.

What was the funniest gift you unintentionally gave or received?

What was your most embarrassing moment while trying out a new hobby?

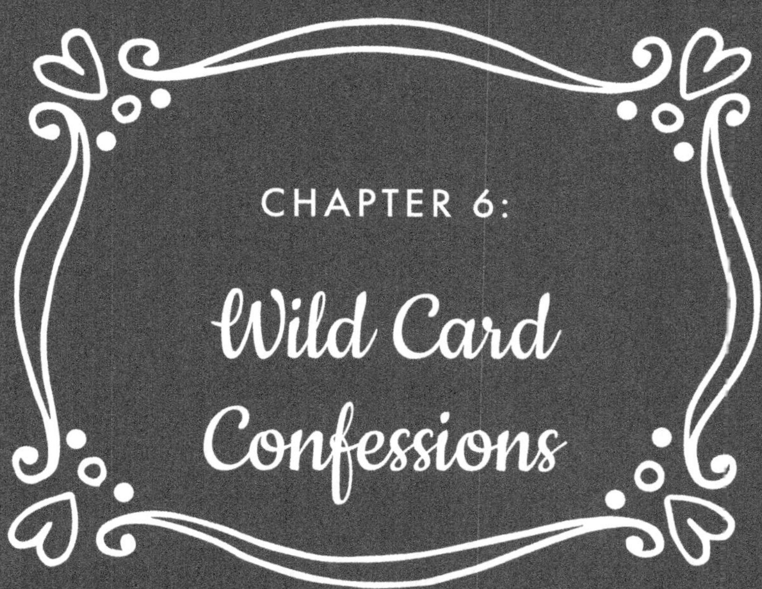

CHAPTER 6:
Wild Card Confessions

What's the most ridiculous thing you've ever believed?

If you could be any fictional character for a day, who would it be and why?

Share the funniest misunderstanding you had about a TV show or movie.

What's the most unusual job you've ever heard of or wanted?

Describe a time you attended a party where you knew nobody and made it fun.

What's the most bizarre thing you've ever eaten on a dare?

Share a story about a time you participated in a strange local custom.

What was the most absurd thing you did on a whim?

Describe your funniest encounter with wildlife.

What's the weirdest dream you remember that made you laugh?

Share the most humorous misunderstanding you had during a trip abroad.

What was the silliest piece of tech you ever tried to use?

Describe the most amusing misadventure you had with a gadget.

What's the funniest mistake you made in a new city?

Share the most bizarre conversation you overheard.

What was the most ridiculous costume you've ever worn?

Describe the funniest way you tried to make a new friend.

What's the most absurd rule you ever had to follow?

Share a story about the funniest thing you did to fit in.

What was the most unusual competition you ever participated in?

Describe your most comical encounter at a zoo or aquarium.

What's the silliest thing you believed about another country?

Share the most humorous mix-up you had with a hotel booking.

What was the funniest animal behavior you've ever witnessed?

Describe the silliest misunderstanding you had about someone's job.

What's the funniest way you tried to learn a new skill?

Share the most comical gift you received without context.

What was the most absurd decoration you put up without realizing it?

Describe the funniest way you tried to solve a problem.

What's the silliest advice you took seriously?

Share your most humorous fail at a sporting event.

What was the most ridiculous thing you did to get out of an obligation?

JUST BETWEEN US:
Yes-or-No Confessions

Have you ever laughed so hard you forgot why you were laughing? Ⓨ Ⓝ

Did you ever smuggle your own popcorn into the cinema in a handbag? Ⓨ Ⓝ

Have you ever faked receiving a call to escape a conversation? Ⓨ Ⓝ

Have you ever mimed a rock concert solo while cleaning? Ⓨ Ⓝ

Did you ever wave at a car just because it honked? Ⓨ Ⓝ

Have you ever tried to unlock the wrong car in a parking lot? Ⓨ Ⓝ

Did you ever nod along to a conversation in a language you didn't understand? Ⓨ Ⓝ

Have you ever greeted someone enthusiastically then realized you didn't know them? Ⓨ Ⓝ

Did you ever mouth the words to a song you didn't know the lyrics to? Ⓨ Ⓝ

Have you ever mentally rehearsed a victory dance for the lottery? Ⓨ Ⓝ

Did you ever accidentally style your hair with something other than hair product? Ⓨ Ⓝ

Have you ever mistaken a mannequin for a person? Ⓨ Ⓝ

Did you ever reply with "You too" when a waiter told you to enjoy your meal? Ⓨ Ⓝ

Have you ever serenaded a pet with a TV theme song? Ⓨ Ⓝ

Have you ever worn sunglasses indoors to feel incognito? Ⓨ Ⓝ

Have you ever claimed a pet's mess as your child's to avoid embarrassment? Ⓨ Ⓝ

Did you ever start giggling at a memory while in a quiet room? Ⓨ Ⓝ

Have you ever forgotten the punchline of your own joke? Ⓨ Ⓝ

Did you ever dust off exercise equipment just before guests arrived? Ⓨ Ⓝ

Have you ever jumped at your shadow? Ⓨ Ⓝ

Did you ever claim to love a dish just to please the host? Ⓨ Ⓝ

Have you ever said "almost there" when you hadn't even left yet? Ⓨ Ⓝ

Have you ever secretly wished to be interviewed by a street reporter? Ⓨ Ⓝ

Have you ever been startled by a balloon popping and acted like nothing happened? Ⓨ Ⓝ

Did you ever convince someone that an obviously false fact was true? Ⓨ Ⓝ

Have you ever worn Christmas socks to a business meeting? Ⓨ Ⓝ

Did you ever improvise a bedtime story so bizarre that it put you to sleep? Ⓨ Ⓝ

Have you ever gestured dramatically with a TV remote as if it were a magic wand? Ⓨ Ⓝ

Did you ever rehearse an acceptance speech for an imaginary award? Ⓨ Ⓝ

Have you ever narrated your pet's thoughts out loud? Ⓨ Ⓝ

Did you ever mismatch your earrings and pretend it was a fashion choice? Ⓨ Ⓝ

Have you ever started a diet only to break it with a midnight snack? Ⓨ Ⓝ

Have you ever hid when someone rang the doorbell and then peeked out the curtains? Ⓨ Ⓝ

Have you ever driven off with a takeaway coffee on your car roof? Ⓨ Ⓝ

Have you ever managed to not kill a houseplant for a whole year? Ⓨ Ⓝ

Have you ever blamed the cat instead of the kids? Ⓨ Ⓝ

Have you ever walked into a room and forgotten why you went there in the first place? Ⓨ Ⓝ

Did you ever laugh at someone's joke only to realize you didn't get it? Ⓨ Ⓝ

Have you ever pretended to be a celebrity to get better service? Ⓨ Ⓝ

Did you ever keep a borrowed pen because you liked it too much? Ⓨ Ⓝ

Did you ever rehearse an argument in your head, just in case? Ⓨ Ⓝ

Have you ever worn mismatched shoes and only noticed halfway through the day? Ⓨ Ⓝ

Have you ever kept the tags on a dress, worn it, and then returned it? Ⓨ Ⓝ

Did you ever get scared by your own reflection in a window at night? Ⓨ Ⓝ

Have you ever laughed at a joke in a movie and realized you were the only one laughing in the theater? Ⓨ Ⓝ

Have you ever put on an accent or pretended to be from somewhere else just for fun? Ⓨ Ⓝ

Have you ever set off an alarm in a store by accident and walked away pretending it wasn't you? Ⓨ Ⓝ

Have you ever gone to greet someone with a handshake and awkwardly switched to a hug at the last second? Ⓨ Ⓝ

Have you ever been caught dancing in your car at a red light? Ⓨ Ⓝ

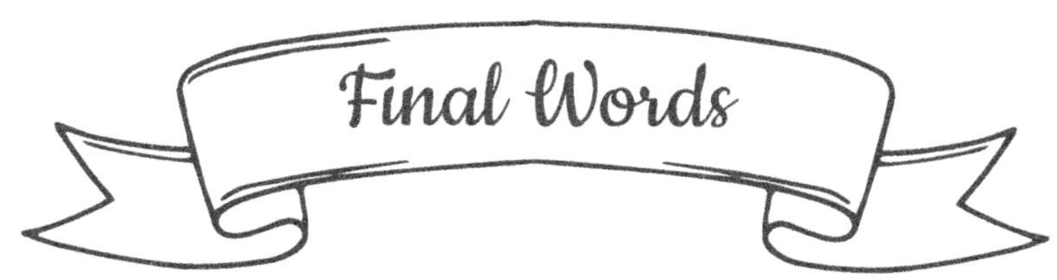

As you close this book, think about the many stories you've written in it. Each one is a different part of your life as a mom. This book is more than just a collection of memories; it's a showcase of your resilience, joy, and love.

Let these pages be a record of all the good and bad things that have happened to you. As you pass this on, remember that it holds the love, happiness, and lessons that make you who you are.

For every laugh and honest moment we've had together on this journey, thank you. Live, love, and laugh with all your heart. Cheers to the memories and stories that are still to come. Don't hold back on telling your stories—they're a gift to the next generation.

Afterthoughts

Made in the USA
Las Vegas, NV
19 August 2024

94122993R00063